Perfect Hurt

Perfect Hurt

Bradford Gray Telford

WAYWISER

First published in 2009 by

THE WAYWISER PRESS

14 Lyncroft Gardens, Ewell, Surrey KT17 1UR, UK
P.O. Box 6205, Baltimore, MD 21206, USA
www.waywiser-press.com

Managing Editor
Philip Hoy

Associate Editors
Joseph Harrison   Clive Watkins   Greg Williamson

A CIP catalogue record for this book is available from the British Library

ISBN 978-1-904130-34-5

Printed and bound by
Cromwell Press Group Ltd,Trowbridge, Wiltshire

for Julie Agoos

Acknowledgements

Some of the poems in this book, often in slightly different versions, first appeared (or will appear) in the following publications:

American Literary Review: "Some Useful Formulas"; *Birmingham Poetry Review*: "Portrait of the Artist's Mother in the Car"; *Bloom:* "Cercis cadanensis var. texensis"; *Borderlands:* "Talking Points"; "Testimonial"; "Case Study"; "Definitions and Exclusions"; "Attachments"; "Risk Transfer"; "For Further Information"; *Carquinez Review*: "*Das Fugue der Kunst*"; "Last Song"; *Diner*: "Vous"; *Eclipse*: "The Woman Who Was Not Matisse"; *Edison Review*: "The Open Book"; *Harpur Palate*: "A Partial Genealogy of Spoken Waves"; *Hawai'i Review*: "The Conversation"; *Hayden's Ferry Review*: "Paulownia tomentosis"; "Regarding a Backsplash"; *Inkwell*: "At the Theatre"; *Nassau Literary Review*: "Portrait of a Memory of a Portrait"; *Oasis:* "Three Biographies"; *Phantasmagoria*: "Melia azederach"; "The Gemstone Globe"; *Southwest Review*: "Portrait of the Artist's Mother at the Analyst"; *Southwestern American Literature*: "Two in One"; "Night and Day Labor"; *Tampa Review*: "Dramatic Monologue in the Voice of the Low Mound from Samuel Beckett's *Happy Days*"; *Zone 3*: "First Death."

Contents

Contents

Perfect Hurt

The Old Master

A holy theatre not only presents the invisible but also offers conditions that make its perception possible.

– Peter Brook

At the Theatre

*A kind of warmth towards one's fellow men is essential –
an understanding of the contradictions in man, and that he
is a suffering creature but not one to be scorned.*

– Jerzy Grotowski

At the Theatre

– for Darin Ciccotelli

We went to the Marinsky on an evening in late June.
Our box hung high above the pit, an expectation.
The conductor bowed. The English horn spoke Russian.
Curtain up on Chinese lantern, Chinese moon.

*

I wondered about the cherubs, what had they seen?
Had they tired in the plaster, their paint and gilt wings?
What bores an angel more – violence or beauty?
Why bother when the program changes nightly?

*

I go to the theatre to forget I'm at the theatre.
I go to the book to forget about the shelf.
I go home to remember I'm a stranger.
I go to you. Remember me. Forget myself.

*

We didn't know what we were seeing.
The chorus sang of nature. A shepherd mentioned grace.
Bulbs flickered in the wings – sheet lightening.
Gobo net the stage in gold-green lace.

*

The actors churned these foam-core scrolls.
They looked like deco-fenders. They were supposed to be waves.
Theatre happens in the brain's soft coils.
They behave the way a churning sea behaves.

*

I was nine – a thirty minute Czech operetta.
Children, wolves, a storm, a stalled train.
The children wanted out, the wolves wanted better
than the wind and the snow and the Czech refrain.

*

I go to the theatre the way Frost went to the woods.
Often I don't like it. But I do feel better.
I work for the theatre the way Rilke worked for Rodin
what with his cold and attitude and thin, bad sweater.

*

The shepherd wanted nothing – that's his job.
The kingdom wanted peace. The drunkard out of jail.
The set designer: more gold, more silver foil.
The emperor would catch the nightingale.

*

Art may be a meeting between a man and his work.
Once there he speaks – he plumbs the heart of "is."
A moon will glow. A deer will learn to walk.
There is no self without artifice.

Vous

An American and a Russian meet in line outside Peterhof.
It's hot, the sky is pink smoke – a moment ago, fireworks.
Now a military band, police dogs, ice cream and chef.
In stalls of dolls a Bush within Madonna wrapped in Marx.
The pair rock on their heels as if warming up or calming down.
Already they've talked through Tsars and Nazis. Lunch.
They so want to see it they can't wait for it to be done.
One of them resolves they pass their time in French.
It's easier than either of them could have imagined.
The simple past and present – everything effortless, true.
Brothers, bad jobs, good movies, what they did over the weekend.
They stick to the formal/plural "you."
The line is slow. Then it stops. Suddenly it moves fast.
Love is kind of like this at first.

Dramatic Monologue in the Voice of the Low Mound from Samuel Beckett's *Happy Days*

— Oh I know you were never one to talk, I worship you

A difficult vantage, one
in which the author excelled.
I was it – his strong-silent type.
A *kvetchy* world. But how he *kvelled*

about my look, my height, my speech
with no word, my grace without wit.
A molehill made from his tall mountain:
frank, sincere, full of shit

or shit itself. What can I say?
I was grateful for the work.
They shoveled me to the mark;
my job? be still, half-burke

the old broad while she spewed
her wretched incidentals:
tabloid, toothpaste, mirror, toy gun.
Loamy, I whetted her genitals,

trickled down her swollen leg
to puddle in the shoe
she claimed she'd bought on sale.
Life is art. It's what you do,

it's who you are, but it's never
quite what you would think or feel.
I think I feel okay with this.
It's taken time, taken a real

Dramatic Monologue in the Voice of the Low Mound
from Samuel Beckett's Happy Days

and sustained effort and lately
I've been recalling that jump
in act II where the lights bump up
and everyone gasps: the frump

is up to her neck as opposed
to her size-18 waist.
She acts, acting like I'm not there.
But she knows me, knows my taste

as it sidles around her jowl,
lubricates her lips and parts south,
ripens up and down her spine
before exploding in her fat mouth –

forgive me. I worked hard,
was haughty and perhaps proud
and, tragic or not,
she and her bad hat *were* loud

especially in those moments
of e-fucking-ternal pause.
I hated the attention.
I loved the applause.

And love is what gives
while art is what returns
a vacant stare, her blink,
my blank. It burns –

Three Biographies

Contemporary

He grew up in a past-imperfect tense
teeming with more versions of events

than an above average crime scene.
The house was large, well kept – so clean

were all the skeletons they shivered
from the lack of dust. Often they gathered

in their jam-packed closets –
among the over-and-unders, the dirndls and dinner jackets –

clattering their million bones together,
a quiet hum, an air-conditioner.

Classical

Dear Cassandra: in art and clairvoyance
be courageous. Pick your audience.

Arrive early. Stay late. Drop the (please) hysteria.
Roll over. Play dead. Don't play Peoria.

Look good. Look away. Leap before you look.
The film is always bad. But better than the book.

Win friends. Speak truth. Act (dear god) like you mean it.
Influence gazillions for fun and for profit.

Tits, ass, teeth, leg – all of it, your bright future.
I, your biggest fan, can hardly wait –

– Clytaemnestra.

Romantic

Here the great whale is turning, rolling over
in his mind, barnacled in black and ochre,

hungry for the sea, to hunt that craft he launched
some years ago before the future lurched

headlong into the future. If the boat
was caught, was now breaking up on a bite

of rocks, would that whale come about, click
and trill, unclench its blowhole eying the crack

or fallen sheet and then move on like weather?
Time is an old child hunting down its mother.

The Woman Who Was Not Matisse

This is the story of the woman who was not Matisse.
I knew her doctor husband, both her daughters – there were no
    sons.
What there was was design, execution, a white Maltese.
And there was a garden: crape myrtle, potted dill. Caladiums.

Caladiums were for Texas for they flourished in the heat.
The dill was for Russia – it drank a lot and needed shade.
A patio in brick, slivered with koi, good teak.
A Baltic ivy trellis in a green-black-black-green braid. *Braid*.

You want a story fine I'll tell you a story.
Her daughters were choices, as was her husband, ditto her black
    clothes.
Ditto each wingback the spine of each book the light the
    rosemary
the floating iron pots on one of two steel stoves.

So everything was perfect and everything was grand.
I'd never seen a thing like it and was half in love.
Her rigor – her edge – her black eye – her white fierce hand.
So many of us alive not knowing how to live!

But in her house there was no color. In her house, no art.
Light woods, dark woods, black-white marble tile.
Silverspined books by Proust and by Sartre.
But no print, no watercolour and no (no, God no) oil.

One day the daughter's harp had been refurbished and delivered.
The inlaid soundbox. The curved blonde shoulder. The ravishing
    neck.
And the woman made them take it away when she discovered
all the pedals re-felted warm pink instead of black-black. *Black*.

Later the daughter told me over drinks what had happened.
One day thirty years ago the woman made a choice, a kind of
    barter.
She'd put away her paint, drawered her work, banked her stipend.
For life was short and hard. And art was long. And harder.

She'd realized she wasn't Matisse. What more do you want?
She knew it would be better. Real life. With different dreams.
And this will happen to you and will happen to me or maybe it
    won't.
The house has been in magazines.

A Partial Genealogy of Spoken Waves

– For Nan Worman and j. Kastely

beyond the reach of words
– Sophocles

I have two friends – both reading the same tragedy.
One friend's a philosopher; the other a retired dancer.
They both like wine and travel. Both work in the academy.
Both of them will ask a question with a question and an answer.

The philosopher was a medic. Two full tours. Vietnam.
The dancer, upon-retirement, became a top-notch Hellenist.
The dancer, upon a *battement,* broke her hip. *Trop grande.*
The philosopher, while a medic, became a (hurried, bloody) optimist.

The philosopher reads from how it works to how it feels.
It doesn't, surprise-surprise, feel good in any way.
The dancer reads from how it feels to how it works. She feels
there's work to do on how she feels about the play.

The dancer, she walks fine despite all her injuries.
Years and years of treatment and she's not even done yet.
The philosopher, he talks in these wry, wry similes –
academic politics? *Like Crimp, like Laos. Like Tet.*

And the play? It's about pain, about time, about what on earth to do.
Whatever can be said and to what kind of spirit.
There is an island, there is a when, is a how. An almost-who.
There is a soul-tree that has fallen and there's no one left to hear it.

No one but a reader, maybe. Okay, maybe an audience.
Maybe a moment shatters on stage and then it's done.
Philosopher, Dancer – maybe they shudder and wince
as a man undergoes his birth – his birth as No One –

undergoes self cracked clean and sheared off the body,
leaving self to trickle and ooze and then dissolve into the sea
where waves hammer the blank beach – *pappapappapai* –
waves and waves. Not dying. Artistically.

Dream House

If I am host at last
It is of little more than my own past.
May others be at home in it.

– James Merrill

The Open Book

for my father

There is one remaining thing between us –
a cord, our nylon umbilicus

anchored to this cracking granite womb.
The mountain is a mother or a tomb

depending where you drive your pitons in
or whether we can thread your bowline

quickly through my harness. If we'd time
enough to think on it we might do well to climb

the peak in abstract terms. Reality.
Harsh. So little room for irony

when strung some sixty feet above a floor
of broken scree – and what could be more

inviting than such dandles and delays
when one of us frenetically belays

the other up this pitch, the Open Book,
as it is popularly known? We hook

each carabiner through each ring as if
it were our final gesture on this face, massive,

more ambiguous than its name suggests,
more slide than surface, yielding fewer footrests

than handholds and those mere crannies: wide
enough for fingers (crammed an inch inside).

Excerpts from a Dream House

The Conversation

We were drinking Diet Coke and talking about our dream house.
Inside: Birdseye maple, concrete floors, pin-spots, his-and-his and
     his-and-his.
Outside: rot, weeds, jays on a soon-to-be-downed wire:
design within nature within desire and desire.

I drew a box and you drew a box and we had two boxes.
My father always said *build more house than you think you can*
     afford.
You like color and comfort and nothing too weird.
I like hundreds of rooms – big, empty as Texas.

We kept at it with crayons and rulers and colored papers.
I showed you mine: stick figures, smiley faces, lots of big orange
     hair.
You said you were frightened of the pet purple monitor lizards.
You kissed me and we made love for an hour.

Then you drew a bedroom with ivory walls, bark trim, one
     spectacular window.
Ten steel clocks that showed the season and the minute.
Maybe I would quit smoking. Maybe you would win the Lotto.
We closed our eyes and made our bed and slept in it.

Two in One

We closed our eyes and made our bed and slept in it.
We dreamed different dreams though we shared the same body.
In my dream a large blue bowl fat with red grapefruit.
In yours – tile the green of soul, the green of big-island Hawaii.

Our one chest rose and fell and rose and fell.
Our one heart kicked our blood in ¾ time.
Our one brain ballooned into a blown glass bell.
Our one mouth muttered *kashepvabiffavime*.

The bell was hot. Then it cooled. Then, of course, it shattered.
Everywhere fragments small and brilliant as märchen.
Everything sharp and color-soaked with everything that mattered.
We gathered up each piece for our mosaic in the kitchen.

Regarding a Backsplash

We gathered up our shards for the mosaic in the kitchen.
I sorted them by shape while you hand-mixed a caramel grout.
I called you "groutiful." And you were. And I was smitten.
You said you'd always grout me. "Nuh-uh, no way – " "No grout."

I picked up a piece. "Oh. God," you said. You said, "it just so ...
    gleams."
You said anything more perfect would just be wrong.
You said we were making beauty from the fragments of our dreams.
"Keats," you said, "and Oprah say that's how to get along."

"Maybe," I said, "it is the shape and color of my love for you."
The color? 'Iridescent Rainbow.' The shape: a four pointed five-
    point star.
A broken figure – breaking toward the real, the true.
"No grout it's beautiful. No grout exactly what we are."

You said "The fifth point is invisible because it's the future."
"It's there. We know it. Only we just can't see."
You kicked me the bucket as I velveted the hammer.
"I'll do the future. You, the present – please – carefully."

I tamped those four points gently in the grout.
You built a fifth: blue agates, shales, a thong of hammered tin.
That night my poor star jimmied loose and then fell out.
That night my future came and put it back again.

Night and Day Labor

Next day we started on the floors with George and sweet, sweet Tim.
Both of them a week off crack and a day, they said, off tina.
Surly, late, refugee-thin.
50 bucks for their car outside some Motel Pasadena.

Took less than an hour to tear up our old shag.
A joke about smoking Carpet Fresh then poor Tim started crying.
Shut your fucking hole ... my last fucking bag ...
George was tired of Tim and Tim was tired, so tired of dying.

Two years earlier their brilliant spring bash –
George proud of his trayed salmon, of Tim, his carved moldings
    and shelves.
Now they needed cash, *CASH!*
They broke for "lunch." We did the floors ourselves.

Portrait of the Artist's Mother in a Banquette

Luncheon at Chester's. Melting aspic
shimmies on the porcelain,
the rolls snug in their basket
like a dray of rich orphans.

"We do as we are able."
Teeth and jewelry glint like sand
as gloves begin to crumb the table.
"You will have to understand:

when I love a thing I feed it."
Laughter crackles. Booth
of widows. Several lawyers fidget.
"It is the blank inside the truth

that turns us into stones."
Models drift among the aisles,
hawk the season's monotones.
"Life's a draggled braid of trials.

Life's a turn of screws and phrase."
Flurries slam against the window.
Harpists thrum a polonaise.
"I am lonely as a shadow.

But shadows are no mystery."
Chester tallies up the bill.
A waiter frowns egregiously.
"I'm a handmaid to my will."

Black cars idle at the curb.
Valets stoop to hold the door.
The duckling was, in fact, superb.
The day is grand. And more is more.

Portrait of the Artist's Mother at the Analyst

The mountains are lovely. The people are not.
And life's a longish novel short on plot

that folds, unfolds in delicate vignettes
of men and women, beef or fowl. *Sos. Yets.*

That's what I know and what I know can kill.
I know the mountains, know their sad vaudeville

of beauty much like most people I've known
whose lives encase them like the icy chrome

you see on all the better mountaintops.
In early evening one drives by bus stops

and almost dies – people – how might they live
without knowing you? *You*? Your need to give

some jonquils or a photo of yourself
to each one of them so each life itself

contracts a mythic sheen while clammy love
evaporates like those thin clouds above

my mountains each spring. I have yet to meet
the person I'll become, whom I shall greet

with that love I've long withheld from others.
I am in hopes that one of us recovers.

Portrait of the Artist's Mother in the Car

She would drive herself to ruin
not to drive herself at all along
these avenues, white as aspirin.

Oh the sun – it is a cabochon
and she alights, triumphant,
a youngish Dido repairing to the back lawn

and her gazebo's latticed quotient:
crape myrtle, ash, mimosa, willow, mint iced tea,
her plated tongs, her succulent

green pears, brown almonds and brie,
her beveled cobalt salver,
her children rimming the fishpond calm as topiary.

And she would drive harder,
faster, stringing days and lives and fears,
her triple choker,

auctionable black pearl years,
while the past she hordes, a delicate jade
too brittle for these atmospheres,

more beautiful for the cracks that fusillade
into the fleshy stone
whose scene depicts a woman presently inlaid

against herself, alone,
driving through November to the shut-up house
she will not call her own.

Four Trees

Melia azederach

When we cut back
your mother's chinaberry tree
she didn't quite cooperate,
didn't go peacefully.

Storms were coming in.
A storm was rolling out.
I Googled her.
I like to know about

a thing before I do
it harm. *Pride-of-India,*
Texas Umbrella, Persian Lilac,
Bead Tree and *Japonica* –

a name for every home.
A crime for every alias.
I clicked her yellow fruit –
rock-hard, poisonous –

cut her leaflets – *toothed, blue-green*
and toxic – dragged along her bark –
a *curative though deadly*,
pasted *the buff, hallmark*

fissures wrenched tight
across her purpled torso
elongating her pain,
a late El Greco

(though each spring she'd burst
in *drooping lilac panicles)*.
Your mother wasn't well.
Sport utility vehicles,

two of them next door
plus a brand new fence,
the storm, her terrible cough,
impeccable evidence

that the dead limb –
one of three in the trunk's braid –
would cleave off easy
(wrong – again). I was afraid.

Lyric and decorative
foreign-born *Melia,*
a transplanted Ruth,
invasive, diligent Medea

wild as the bow saw bit
into her soft back.
We got her down,
her snapping twigs black

with your blood and my blood,
the sheeted sweat, the flecks of skin,
a ritual we'd do once
and be done with and then

you watched me jump.
I crushed her spine.
We left her by the road.
What's yours is mine

and what is mine may well
be yours. I think. We're both givers.
It was late.
We looked down: ants, carpenters

sifting their wreckage,
dirt, dried pith, broken phloem,
pale larvae clamped tight in black jaws.
There – there was the poem.

Four Trees

Cercis cadanensis var. texensis

My mother's favorite photograph of me –
I am seven or eight, plaid shorts, shirt – both cranberry –

bowl haircut, black socks, a double-tongued brass grommetted belt
and crepe-souled oxford lace-ups (black) in which I felt

able to climb just about anything and did.
I, climber. That dirty kid

in the neighborhood with clouds in his eyes,
bark under his skin, bark scabbed into his knees, his pale thighs

and itching for a purchase high above the brown composite shingles.
A loner with a view, a thought. In my pocket, Skittles,

maybe a book and always a plan
to stay up and away as long as I could and can

you blame the climber for inhabiting this idea
of bodark? Of live oak? Of wax-leaved magnolia?

Up high and loving it – the pure good
of leafy being, letting the clammy wood

bore into my back I, for a couple of hours,
watched tiny construction men fit steel girders to the towers

rising among the dozen or so white and yellow cranes,
rising to the call, it seemed, of their Utopian names:

Four Trees

Electronic Data Systems, Medical City,
Trammel Crow Village, Park Central Two, Plaza Infinity –

I could reach out my hand. I could almost create.
I could order and reorder the entire state

of Texas as it boomed and busted wide into my blue sky
while far below me the wishbone double-y

of freeways slamming together and splitting apart
crashed and rolled past True Value Hardware and Abdul Mini Mart

sounding, my mother said, sort of like an ocean.
"The Gulf, the gulf," she said, her diction

flat as Midland or clogged, at times, as traffic –
motioning me into the frame of her Instamatic

with its glacier-blue flash-cube,
each of its four sides framing a magnesium tube

which would – at the push of a button – both explode and be
        contained.
Earlier it'd rained

and it must have been the spring.
My mother's favorite redbud tree was hemorrhaging

from each of its hundred faithful limbs,
as were most of her other prized specimens:

tulip trees, dogwoods, the bearded wisteria
all skirted with brick and pine fence to keep those Oklahoma

old-field-trash neighbors
out, out of our manicured half-acre's-

worth of doable paradise.
Nothing grand or showy. Comfortable. "Nice

enough," my father said.
My mother is arranging me – "your arms, your head –

look up, look out – "
I could probably care less. This tree is small, about

three times my mother's height
and I am only seen and cannot see. "That's *right* – "

she snaps and flashes. Snaps and flashes again.
The photograph is in a silver frame on her secretary in the den

beside the inkwell and the miniature Tiffany safe.
She says it's "Brad and Flowering Judas – which is the Tree of Lost
    Faith."

Four Trees

Albizia julibrissin Durz

My father always said that only God
could kill you. So. I focused on your crotch.
A pick-axe first. Then a ball-peen hammer.
Then turpentine the color of the scotch

my father saved for company. I forget
what else. You had that air the persecuted
get – you know, part *come hither*, part *oh well* –
and while I should have been electrocuted

five-times over by that oven-sized
reflector lamp, the rotting wires half-hooked
into your skin, I kept after you,
tended you, *mon oeuvre*, until you looked

as if you'd hemorrhaged paint, epoxy, glue,
three different shades of caulk, fists of chrome tacks
with fiddleheads of reddish, black-brown nails
erupting from your trunk. These are the facts

that hang off me just like your envelopes
of fruit, dead-letter packages, oh seed –
parched, dangerous, itching in the wind,
yakkety-yakking, taunting me – you'd need

a girdling and I would need to clap
a rope saw (which I stole) around your shins,
your calves, easing my will into your soft
soft flesh like the argument that begins,

after that first cut, to seem voluptuous –
that offers consolation and a cure –
that sprouts bouquets of pom-pommed
inflorescences to quietly lure

the soul, its compound eyes and hairy feelers,
out of warm darkness and into the light –
the better to see you with, my dear –
your papery bark, my rigorous bite,

the thrilling metal of my logic
shanked around the torso of your flesh, your drive.
My father toasted me. We moved that year
and took God with us, took him alive –

Four Trees

Paulownia tomentosis

By then the forsythias had dropped their gold show
to bushel and peck
the walks and bedded ponds of Mercer County
with a green and general optimism –

so too the crocuses, of course, and their exactingly small retreat

and all the azaleas, the weeping cherries, old fists
of wisteria had by then and too soon
given and given up
their white and purple ghosts
to jade and emerald an all-purpose June,
a time of early lush, a time of warm before the time of heat,
time leafing into a tired mind
such subtleties as could not be complete
without great change or greater knowledge

and if you've ever looked and I mean really looked at green you know
the beautiful and the impossible and so

from my third floor balcony on Nassau Street I'd simply stopped.
I'd learned the definition of "enough."

I had watched the tulips *tim-ber!* in the garden.
I'd watched the news on a friend's old TV.
Had read up on the spirit's meaningful unquiet and
none of it, nada, nope, nothing to do with me,

any of it and so from that balcony
I smoked and wondered *why, why summer?*

Why? I asked the dead-
as-if-staged-in-a-Beckett-one-act Empress tree,
the last third of it visible from my balcony's perch
inclining to spindle and lurch
out of my front yard and into June's sky
like a burnt coat rack salvaged from a gutted manor's mudroom,
     god we talked –

the dead by choice to the dead by chance –

as the tree's leaves curled up and cracked ugly-brown as old
     placemats
only to then and one-by-one
detach and husk the glittering-wet green-silver ground –

I looked away,
I veered inward to my summerless heart
as 5000 empire gowns trumpeted all her black branches
before letting billow-sway such pink, *pink* mazurkas that I

I with a start looked back
                    and it hurt.

The Gemstone Globe

As usual you have given me the world
and as usual I've got my complaints
like these non-tarnish brass legs oddly curled
out at the foot suggesting in their slants
any number of origins but nothing
certain – rat-claw, Dutch, Dutch angular, drake
or mongrel dog-paw – and while the compass
needle planted in the stretcher points, quivering
towards its true north, it would be a mistake
to think this world and its decorative Atlas

entirely ideal for one another.
Love. Again. Stuck on a goofy pedestal
thanks to a late-night lapse in judgment, Mother,
that and dumb luck, for it is The Beautiful,
A Globe of Many Colors, fraught with lines
of longitude and latitude that weave
their gilt cage of pure perspective shot through
soft continents and imperial blue-
black seas – itineraries leap to mind –
where you're going, who with, when you might leave

and if you plan on coming back. I'm glad
you travel. Time was when this stone-cold *terra
lapidosa* might have been it, the sad
and lonely *que* on life's *sera-sera*.
How many years comprised your long dark night
in your television's blue-rinse glow?
You, you – buried among your lacquered fans
and cloisonné boxes in a twilight
of national anthem, test pattern, then snow.
You were not happy. You'd made other plans

or perhaps other plans made you. Who knows?
One day a wall came down. Everything changed.
Everything stayed the same. You bought good clothes
and tried the world, even as it rearranged
itself into its current blur of faction
(funny that they've set it all in stone
or iridescent abalone shell,
white jade, agate, tiger-eye, and lapis ocean
lapping, glittering, wild in gold-flecked foam).
When your world was ending whom did you tell?

Or did you bank and turn on your own axis,
gleaming with the knowledge that end is all
the world can ever do? We lose. Our practice
makes it perfect. I use non-aerosol
organic cleanser once a week (or when
I can remember), paying special mind
to Greece, Iran, America, those three
republics carved from Turquoise, China-mined,
I'm certain, in Tibet – where the air's thin,
the labor cheap, the plateau broken, chalky –

Perfect Hurt

... there you feel free.

– T. S. Eliot

Portrait of a Memory of a Portrait

October morning, 1982,
my father perched above his subject
fixing, angling, goose-necked like an instrument
probing the filthy godlet with his view-

finder, cropping the gratuitous, lenses
grinding to a shutter-click, the zoom
snarfling what it came for. *Namaste boom-boom.*
'My god seeks your god. And candy too,' hence his

willingness to pose, the clasped hands, that stare.
Past timberline, the Kingdom of Nepal,
where dollops of geography fall
like active culture on the tongue, in Pher-

iche, at Namche-Bazaar, up from Lukla,
down from Kala Patar (a land where north
is up and down, right and wrong, back, forth)
we sought the Greater Truth. They gave us hoopla.

Monks in Tyangboché deployed three horns long
as minivans whose proud vibrations ploughed
into the valley walls while this shag cloud
ripped above our heads – prayer flags – the throng

crackling like gunfire blowing to tatters
pleas for long life, healthy children, good crops –
the north wind out of China never stops –
so these frayed angels tend our earthly matters

capably as hospice workers, that
is what I'm sure of. That is what I'm told.
Inside: Buddhas, bodhisattvas, and gold –
gold slicking the walls, the beams, the mat

on which a pink lama sat brooding, staring
at a Wheel of Life wedged tight in the breach
of Death's open jaws. Amazing. Each
of six fangs a prong, our Tiffany setting

where merrily we roll along, oh, art gives –
keeps intact and at bay, is here but not now,
now (forever) so far away, how
they come up with it God knows. Look – cursives

of gilt ice uncurling as if to blow
forever off that mandala's depiction
of the Great Mountain, the summit of fiction
whose own summit cradles, they say, the basso

tectonic *Ohm*. For people who believe,
it is the sacred sound. For people lost,
losing or later found to have glossed
over their whole lives and now they grieve

the glossing like you grieve your neighbor's wife –
wondering how he gets along without her,
worrying, hoping he's a drunk, devout, or
blessed with Alzheimer's and that afterlife

it brings (violence, diapers). Last year
you watched their brittle winter lean-to
cough and falter down the glazed avenue,
her blue rinse freezing to her skull, a tear

of caking spittle on his cheek, "the A-
frame couple," you muttered, "on six legs
at evening – four flesh, two wood" and so begs
that old riddle: we die. Good. Does love stay

lingering like Indian summer? like one
of two shit-faced ushers at a closed cash bar?
like a Palm Springs hooker (once a child-star)
fondling his cha-cha's white oblivion?

Like Demeter I have scoured this cold planet,
bloodying my fingers on these hard clays,
sifting for a lost word or daughter days
and nights and days. My daughter-word – to know that

surely she's alive, her glistening *I am*
that licks one expertly crosshatched and shaded
beaux-arts eye, incandescing ideal hatred,
love, or nothingness – here, I'll diagram –

sketching out the pupil I vein the white,
hook the lashes and now box that small void
where light ricochets and splashes rhomboid,
hexagonal, wrenching and clear and all night,

all night I drink and dial my draftsman friends
who, to a draft, believe in such a word
(here's to the elegant, the disinterred,
the common grave of lost technique), one that ends

with a flourish, an "e", *accent aigu*,
one that ushers in the age, expels
the moneychangers, bids sweet-low farewells
to poetry, Hollywood, life, what-have-you,

one perfect word. Do you know what I mean?
A man I loved wanted to die
and come back as a wave whereas I, I
favored a go as that whispering scene

from the Zapruder Film, you know, that moment
where she leans in like she's snuggling for
the out-of-town cameras right before
his head cracks back as if struck by a brilliant

idea. Frame number 313. My father –
young, perfect, horn-rimmed, starched white lab coat –
was there that day, at Parkland, and I quote:
"A wall of frightened people, the corridor

hushed with work, quietly panicked, typical,"
gurney rolling by, my Father looking down –
a black cave gashed open temple-to-crown –
"your average big city public hospital."

My mother laid my brother in his crib.
My father laid his clipboard on a table.
Cronkite lifted off his glasses, barely able,
agonizing ad-lib to ad-lib

and that's the way it was. The way it is
on larger prints you can detect a line,
crooked, meandering through the wet shine
of the boy's brown eye, suggesting ridges,

shelves of granite, lips of ice and time,
a hinting at a thing as old or older
than any beauty, any lorn beholder.
My father gave me mountains. I must climb.

Self-Portrait on a Need-to-Know Basis

Talking Points

I feel I am being ironed, it doesn't burn at all.
– Tomaž Šalamun

It's about compression. It's about love
conquering most but not all. It's about
misery loving company throughout
much of our shared history and above
all else it's time laid out like picked-over
hors d'oeuvres – the tired fruit, the sweaty cheese,
a lone fly catching a buzz off the empties,
stray feathers off a white ostrich boa –
"what was her name? she came with him? was she
a she? a he? a shim?" and other questions
gather, publicists to these small rooms,
pitching, flakking that it's all about me
staked out in semi-formal tensions:
death, not dying, life as it resumes –

Testimonial

Immortality is preferable in this life

Any discussion of my death presumes
I lived once and was happy doing so.
It's hard to tell. It was ages ago.
Briefly I dwell on it in volumes
I and II of *Period Costumes,*
a work attributed to me although
I don't remember writing it but oh
do I remember wiping down the heirlooms
of one unwished-for past (the photographs,
the ticket stubs, the hatreds, the fey laughs)
and finally getting it – that as a man
expired I was to record with some feeling
what he knew of life when he began
to forget who he was (and/or die trying).

Case Study

If I had called, and he had answered me.
– Job 9:16

There once was a man who forgot that dying
was a choice, who eventually forgot
to die altogether. His children thought
him spiteful or, *peut-etre*, lazy, citing
myth, biology, habit, good taste, voicing
grave concern about his stamina. "Not
that we don't love you," said that hateful snot,
his daughter, "not that we don't care" a mincing
son halfheartedly allowed while his friends,
such as they were, found themselves at loose ends
dying one after the other without
even a word from him. Not *god, goodbye*
nor any coveted or talked-about
invectives hurled at loved ones, ocean, sky.

Definitions and Exclusions

Thus there arises a curious contradiction of words.
– St Augustine

Of course the weather is a metaphor
for weather in that *deluge, blanket, breath*
of, raging, higher, dog days, wetter, four
breathe *life* (itself a metaphor for death
by freak desire) into that old campaign
to bracket our now and thus return to it –
making journey out of destination Pain –
making one-time-chance-encounter pure habit
which makes for harder breaking than both heart
and wild horse. At seven I asked my Father
for a horse. "I'll buy you pictures" (art
will save us) "of a horse." And what odd bother,
this having been saved, like time, like string,
like money for a rainy day. *Ka-ching* –

Attachments

Of course there always will be darkness
but I realize now something inhabits it.
— Mark Z. Danielewski

Faith? Forgiveness? Money. For it is never
the most important thing but always
the second most important thing. Always
it is a giver and the gift that never
gives so much as trades, negotiates, never
blinking, neither fraught nor flurried, always
cool, erect, in spats and cutaway, always
urging our complete surrender and never
had we given it a second thought
until that day when money sealed its border,
broke off talks, expelled our last ambassador
or next-to-last. We cried, cried wolf, half-fought,
let slip our lapdogs of war, then stood
our gift horse way up Vine, past Hollywood —

Risk Transfer

He's going to make you some shirts.
– James Salter

A Hollywood ending is that which should
not happen happening to those who often
don't deserve whatever the glad or good-
enough tidings offered in the proven
three-act formula. Fine. But then what
of Hollywood beginnings? Stretched and gouached
like pearly-pastel abstracts with the not-
so-far-fetched theory going Fortune sloshed
her roadie on us just the other day
as evidenced by [your example here]
authenticating life – a prized Manet
at auction: gavel, gasp, a muffled cheer
among The Great whose goods get tagged and crated,
ever to be loved, lived-through, duplicated –

For Further Information

I think about my work every minute of the day.
– Jeff Koons

We want to be loved for what we've created –
not for whom nor what we are, not for how
important or precious or devastated
we, at our core, might be, although now-
a-days speculation on this core
would have us all made real by perfect hurt –
our dear gaping uncovered in the desert
outside Taos where the sky and mud floor
of our world give unexpected way
in a thousand-foot drop of sheared basalt
broken like a bottomless argument
into layer, fragment, contour, and fault,
into what we did that molten day
our great rift opened and begat this moment.

The Old Master

In Memoriam, Tadeusz Danielewski
1923-1993

"An actor remembers everything."

If you set out on a journey let it be long
wandering that seems to have no aim groping your way blindly
so you learn the roughness of the earth not only with your eyes
*   but by touch*
so you confront the world with your whole skin

– Zbigniew Herbert

Autorequiem

Los Angeles, 1993

This January's sordid emptiness
                    affronts me. Most things do.
An astronaut or suicide might stare
                    deep in this reductive blue
and think it fine or vaguely sentimental.
                    Trees should look like brains
devoid of lobes, of tissue,
                    clot up like frozen veins
and scratch their open-ended questions
                    on the Santa Ana winds.
Instead the yuccas and the date palms flap –
                    marled absinthic knots of false friends
imploring me to snap, to buckle
                    under diligent re-exposure
to seasonless midwinter's
                    smogged, oblique foreclosure
where the sun cracks back the eye
                    tamps the world into our cornea
and death's the only promise
                    we can keep in California.

First Death

Warsaw, 1931

I was my mother's favorite apparatus –
out of her I grew stiff
and presentable, a marbled acanthus,

a worry stone clutched in her griffe.
I knew my brother was the favorite son –
his hand-embroidered handkerchief

lay crumpled by his tattered Mendelssohn
Elijah – always, always sick,
Tchaikovsky-like, he might have *been* Russian,

compositions thick
with maudlin counterpoints and blooming
brooding swells, he drove all Warsaw frantic

while his breathing
de-crescendo'd: TB wheeze.
Maman had sent me, instrumental foundling

fixed on skinny knees,
I watched hot sweat clef that white face,
watched academic Furies

score their salty rhythms down his chest, his waist.
He sang pure filth, *kurva*
mnie matka ... she listened on the staircase.

And though we never spoke about it after,
still she hummed and still
I hear his music: major. Major –

September

Warsaw, 1939

I guess I was the quintessential "lad."
They said my having little meant I had

it all, this life before me stretching out,
an endless pocket endlessly turned out.

Then planes, fires. Then the first battalion.
Then night and smoke and then mere oblivion

sans teeth sans eyes sans taste everything I
used to sing I used to sing I used to sing.

There

Oświęcim, 1942

To be grown is to be aware
that protocols of hatred
are held more self-evident
than sacred.

Held? Past tense of Hell.
Past-imperfect plausible.
Shifting hatred to a future
wholly inescapable.

The scene? Remarkably Sylvan –
broad meadows cut by foamy creeks,
the air so thick with sheep
you couldn't hear the shrieks

sometimes (of course you could
though you tried not to,
sometimes the silence wolfed,
devoured you).

Players? Mostly Jews.
And Gypsies. Homosexuals.
The occasional criminal.
The stupid intellectuals.

And me? Grand Old Warsaw's
gangly young Resistance.
The first day aloof, big-eared,
cool in my insistence –

I was not a part of this,
I was not among them.
Night. Solitude.
Poison, poison.

Antidote? The Troupe:
seven men on makeshift sets –
Stanislavski skeletons
and tinkling marionettes

we pranced, strung up,
strung along by hunger, by no hope,
expressions fixed, intentions clear
inside the fetid taupe

of those recycled uniforms
in which some recited their *Shema*
while we soliloquized the black boots down,
camping up the light repertoire:

The Clouds and *Lysistrata*.
The Seagull and *Cymbeline*.
Le Bourgeois Gentilhomme.
A Midsummer-Night's Dream.

Audition

London, 1946

I was Prince Hamlet – and was meant to be.
My acting saw me through the war's
abomination, abominable destiny

guided me, absurdity to absurdity
and straight to RADA's venerated doors.
There I *was* Prince Hamlet, turned out to be

the gauntest Dane that they would ever see –
I contemplated *my* skull pocked with the sores
abomination left there especially

for young, impressionable me
before the Russians crushed those Nazi whores
(who loved Prince Hamlet and had meant to be

abominable, a Reiched eternity).
Their parallel to *Hamlet* underscores
annihilation as the destiny

for nations staging history
as if it were farce – a cry, a god of slammed doors –
I am Prince Hamlet. And am meant to be.
Abomination's no fucking destiny.

Art History

Barcelona, 1966

Dalí was a brilliant fake –
no one knew except for me –
I'd filmed him watching Spain explode
beneath the weight of Franco.

No one knew, except for me,
that this could happen to a country.
Beneath the weight of Franco
or similar anomaly

this often happens, and the country
panics, dies, an animal
or similar analogy.
And though there's nothing similar

to the panic of an animal
feeding off its own species,
there's something similar
in the artist's body

feeding his identity
while the world goes up in flames.
The artist's body
dies and dies, his legacy

to the world. *Go up in flames
and which, if any part of me,
will really die?* he asked of me
like I was some blank canvas

which lately didn't startle me.
I'd filmed him watching Spain explode
like it was all a brilliant canvas
even Dalí could not fake.

Salt Song

Provo, 1984

There's something primal in the lake,
the city and the Great Salt Desert.
It assaults the heart in salts that cake
so terribly while the lake, the lake
recedes, recedes – soon salt sand will rake
its waters to a salt-blown quiet,
the salty sound that's vital to the lake –
salt-pity in a Great Salt Desert.

Workshop

Culver City, 1989

The intention was clear but was it clear
enough? What you desire must be as plain
as the nose on your face and then your face
will disappear. An actor is all nose
and haunches in the end – there's nothing else
except objective, coiling like a spring

around his choices, an actor's sole offspring.
The trick: make it new, make it fresh, make-clear.
The trick is not to become someone else
but to be yourself on a different plane,
existing through your senses, through the nose,
the eyes, the skin, then suddenly your face

will split apart and the character's face
shoots out, a gladiolus in the spring.
And as for what will happen next who knows?
Play with it, have fun, relax, try to clear
your throat the way the character would. Plane
your gestures down to mere breathing or else

holler *Come out with your hands up or else!*
Then come out, come out! For you too will face
that terrible moment – to explain
what you are by pure doing – when the spring
snaps-to and the runway is clear
for take off, all that the character knows

resonates beneath the tip of your nose
like radar, and there is nothing else
that matches this ecstatic rapture clear
of great sex or imminent death and face
it – all fine and inspired actions spring
from love or fear of one or both, our plane

of being, as it were, and though we complain
about the scripts, the director who knows
next to nothing, studios that spring
for stars instead of art, something else
entirely keep us here, striving to face
the challenge which at times remains unclear:

to spring upon the world like nothing else
it knows and give that world a dazzling face,
plain as its own, beautiful, and ten times as clear.

Das Fugue der Kunst

Los Angeles, 1992

A student carved this likeness of my head.
He said that wood and people both had souls.
The trick, of course, was in the cadence struck
between the two – the subject driving in,
the medium pushing out so each could hold
the other one at bay, a perfect check
and balance. Music of the eye, he said,
will play forever if you'll only look
each time as if it were your first and last
encounter in the world of the sightline.

The trick, of course, was in the balance struck
between the student's driving in his soul
and pushing out my likeness from soft wood.
My head was full of music when I heard
him say a medium held forever if
and only if the eyes could play like two
imperfect people, each the other's first
and last encounter in their world of sight –
a dart of love, a love that draws its line
as if one look could carve itself in time.

A medium plays itself like music, held
at bay between what people want to see
and what the artist needs to say, and love
is love, imperfect in its cadence. First
it strikes the student on his head and throws
him out of balance, then it carves a line
upon his soul and grafts its wooden subject
(hearts can vanish in a beat of time),
and last, a likeness of the world will trick
his eyes and drive him to encounter it

and it, I said, is beating like a heart
between the student likened to his art
and subjects struck forever out of time.
But counterbalanced on that perfect line
we draw is love – a love we must obey
with all our mediated interplay
of music pulsing from our wooden souls
what with our unstrung tongues, our eyes' f-holes
that resonate with all we see, I said,
while carving up my world inside my head.

Last Song

Los Angeles, 1993

We are nothing but the stories that we tell.
We are all the people that we'll never know.
We are oceans, echoed in a shell.
We are the barren harvests that we sow.
You'd think that I'd be sick of all these saws
by now. I am. But if I had my druthers
I would die to grow sick of more because
we're all dying – and some faster than others.
Our heaven is here, our hell is here, and love –
the bleeding angel of no soul – is here.
It flaps its broken wing, it hangs above
our ground, it whispers in our grave's dirt ear
one name that we forget before it rolls, dives
vanishing beneath the soil of our lives.

Notes

"At the Theatre": *"the Marinsky"* is the Marinsky theatre, the 18th century opera house in St. Petersburg, Russia.

"Dramatic Monologue in the Voice of the Low Mound in Samuel Beckett's *Happy Days*": the epigraph is from Act One.

"A Partial Genealogy of Spoken Waves": *"pappapappapai"* is a transliteration of one of Philoktetes's cries as written in Sophocles's play.

"Testimonial": the epigraph is the first line from an abandoned poem I found in an old notebook.

"First Death": "kurva / mnie matka ..." In Polish, literally, "Fuck me mother ..."

Index of Titles and First Lines

Index of Titles and First Lines

A Note About the Author

Bradford Gray Telford has published work in many journals including *The Yale Review, Ninth Letter, Southwest Review, Bomb, Pleiades, Gulf Coast, Hayden's Ferry Review, Columbia, Laurel Review, Agni, Lyric,* and *Bloom.* For his work on the poetry of Geneviève Huttin Telford recently won the Willis Barnstone Translation Prize, and his translation of Huttin's book *The Story of My Voice* will appear in Fall 2009 from Host Publications. Telford earned an AB from Princeton, an MFA from Columbia, and a PhD in Literature & Creative Writing from the University of Houston, where he won The Verlaine Poetry Prize, two fellowships to the Krakow Poetry Seminar, and the Stella Ehrhardt Memorial & Cullen Fellowship. Currently, he teaches in the Department of English at the University of Houston, where he is a Houston Writing Fellow.